Bexley & Thayer: The Mystery of Santa Claus

Surprising Answers for Curious Kids…

Ed Taylor

Printed in the United States of America

Second Printing

Published by:

Worldwide Santa Claus Network, LLC

ISBN: 978-0-9970013-4-1

Editor: Jessica Vineyard, Red Letter Editing

I spent years helping Santa before I started noticing the clues. Once I did, they just kept coming—each one clearer and more exciting than the last.

Even now, new clues and discoveries continue to unfold, and the adventure never seems to end.

I'm dedicating this book to you—to everyone with a curious heart who wants to uncover the secrets and hidden meanings behind Santa Claus.

What you're about to discover is like finding a hidden door to a world where kindness is a superpower, joy is a natural state of being, and you get to be part of an amazing adventure, making the world a little bit better and brighter every single day!

Contents

Santa's reindeer, teaching them how courage, adaptability, joy, love, and other virtues can guide them through life's challenges and spread the magic of the North Star.

Chapter 5. The Santa Gene

As Bexley and Thayer begin to activate the Santa Gene in others, they learn that the light of the North Star grows stronger through small acts of kindness and connection.

Chapter 6. The Secret of the North Star

Grandpa reveals the deeper meaning of the North Star as the guiding light that helps us live authentically and inspire others to do the same.

Chapter 7. Spreading the Light

Bexley and Thayer organize a Christmas Eve event to bring their community together, where they share the lessons they've learned and pass on the magic of Santa's light.

Chapter 8. The Bigger Reason for a Wish List

Bexley and Thayer learn that writing a wish list helps them to focus their goals, align with their True North, and take meaningful steps toward their dreams.

Chapter 9. The Mystery of the Coal

Grandpa introduces Bexley and Thayer to the deeper meaning of coal, not as punishment but as a challenge to ignite their inner spark and grow.

Chapter 10. He Sees You When You're Sleeping

Grandpa reveals that Santa doesn't watch us in the literal sense; rather, he feels the energy of our actions through the magic of the North Star, which links us all.

Chapter 11. The True Santa Spirit Lives On

Grandpa delivers one last message, reminding Bexley and Thayer that the magic of the North Star connects everyone. He entrusts them with the responsibility of keeping the light alive for future generations.

Bonus Content

Reflection Prompts

Activities

This bonus content is designed to help you discover your own light, follow your True North, and share kindness and joy with others.

Preface

Bexley & Thayer: The Mystery of Santa Claus takes the reader on a captivating journey that uncovers the deeper truths behind the legend of Santa Claus. Blending timeless holiday magic with meaningful life lessons, this tale reimagines the story of Santa and the North Star as symbols of kindness, courage, and connection—a light that lives within us all.

Through this story, Ed Taylor, often referred to as 'Santa' Ed, or That Santa Guy, hopes to show readers experiencing their "Golden Christmas" that the true magic of Santa Claus isn't just in the stories or traditions, it's in the light we all carry within us. By following the symbolic North Star and finding our own True North, we can spread the spirit of Santa Claus every day of the year.

Designed for pre-teen readers yet layered with insights to engage adults, *Bexley & Thayer: The Mystery of Santa Claus* bridges the gap between childhood wonder and growing curiosity of Santa's authenticity. For children questioning the reality of Santa, this story offers a heartfelt, inspiring way to preserve the magic while answering their questions in a way that respects their maturing understanding of the world.

Using rich metaphors such as the North Star, the Santa Gene, and the reindeer virtues, the tale gently guides readers to discover their True North—the kindest and most authentic version of themselves. Santa is reframed as more than just a man in a red suit; he becomes a living symbol of the generosity, connection, courage, and joy we can all share.

Parents will find this story a valuable resource for helping their children transition from believers to helpers. Children will learn that the magic of Santa isn't just something they wait for once a year, it's also something they create by following their own True North, acting with kindness and spreading light to others. Thoughtful writing or discussion prompts and creative activities are included to help readers explore their own True North and discover how they can spread the light of kindness, courage, and joy in their everyday lives.

Whether you're a child looking for answers, a parent seeking to preserve the spirit of the holidays, or simply someone who loves the magic of Christmas, *Bexley & Thayer: The Mystery of Santa Claus* offers an inspiring exploration of how the legend of Santa can transform lives and illuminate the world all year long.

Chapter 1. The Call of the North Star

The snow was falling heavily in the town of Central Point, blanketing the streets in a perfect white silence. Eleven-year-old Bexley sat cross-legged on the living room rug, flipping through an old book her dad had left out. It was one of those

big, dusty books filled with holiday stories—
legends about Santa Claus, his reindeer, and
magical Christmases from long ago.

"Do you think Santa's real?" Bexley asked
out loud, not really expecting an answer.

Thayer, her nine-and-a-half-year-old
brother, sat nearby, munching on a candy cane. "I
mean, he's fun to think about," he said. "But
come on, how would he visit every house in one
night?"

Bexley frowned. "That's what I'm trying to
figure out. Everyone just says, 'It's magic.' But
what does that even mean?"

Before Thayer could reply, a soft knock
sounded from the front door. The sister and
brother exchanged a puzzled glance.

"Who'd be out in this snowstorm?" Thayer
whispered.

Their mom answered the door. It was Grandpa, entering with a smile.

Grandpa's beard was frosted with snow, his cheeks red from the cold. He wore a long, dark coat and carried an old-fashioned leather satchel.

"Today I'm here just to see Bexley and Thayer," he told their mom, his voice warm and friendly.

Their mom smiled as she turned and went into the kitchen. Grandpa stomped the snow off his boots, took off his coat, and entered the cozy living room.

"I was told you've been asking questions about Santa Claus. I thought you might like some answers."

Thayer popped up behind Bexley, his eyes wide. "Is this some kind of joke?"

Grandpa chuckled. "No, not at all. But the answers you're looking for aren't simple. If you're curious, I have a story to tell."

Bexley hesitated. There was something unusual about Grandpa on this night, something both strange and familiar. "Uh, OK," she said, gesturing toward the couch.

Grandpa placed his satchel on the coffee table, smiled at his beloved grandchildren, and pulled a thick envelope from the bag. He set it on the table in front of them.

"Go ahead. Open it," he encouraged.

Bexley carefully slid her finger under the seal and pulled out a piece of parchment. The handwriting was elegant, like calligraphy, and the words shimmered faintly in the firelight as she read.

The magic of Christmas isn't what you think.
If you wish to understand, follow the light.
It begins with the North Star.

"What's this supposed to mean?" Bexley asked, staring at the letter.

Leaning forward, Grandpa said, "It means that the story of Santa Claus is much bigger than you know, much more than a man in a red suit. It's about light, connection, and a kind of magic that lives in all of us."

Thayer squinted at him. "Okay, Grandpa, I know you have always looked like Santa Claus, but how do you know so much about him?"

Grandpa smiled. "You could say I'm one of Santa's human helpers. I've spent many years helping people uncover the truth about Santa Claus. And this evening, I'm here for you two."

"Why us? Why now?" Bexley asked.

"Well, it's not because you're my grandkids, it's because you're now asking the right questions," he said simply. "You're asking questions about what Santa really means. The magic of Christmas needs new Keepers, people who can carry the light forward and keep the Christmas spirit strong all year long."

Grandpa reached into his satchel again and pulled out a small crystal star, shining softly in the light. "Do you know what this is?" he asked, holding it up.

Thayer shook his head no, but Bexley leaned closer. "It looks like the North Star," she said, remembering her astronomy class at school. "The North Pole at the top of the world points to the North Star all the time."

"Exactly," Grandpa said. "The physical North Star is a pretty dim star in the sky, about halfway up from the northern horizon. But our own personal North Star is a symbol of something we all have inside us. It is the guiding light that we can follow toward kindness, generosity, warmheartedness, and truth. Santa's magic starts with following that light."

Bexley tilted her head. "So, you're saying the North Star is . . . inside us?"

"Well, kind of," Grandpa replied. "You have something inside you we call True North. Your True North acts as a compass that points you toward the symbolic North Star. It is the part of you that knows what's right, even when it's difficult to do. Santa's story has always been about being warmhearted, following your True North, and sharing it with others."

Thayer crossed his arms. "Okay, but what about the flying reindeer and the presents? Are you saying all that's not real?"

Grandpa chuckled again. "Oh, the reindeer and the gifts are very real but not in the way you think. They're part of the Santa Claus story because they are symbols of bigger ideas. If you want to understand, you'll need to uncover the rest of the story."

Bexley glanced at Thayer, who nodded. "We're in," she said firmly. "What do we do next?"

Grandpa's smile widened. "You'll follow the clues. This," he said, pointing to the twinkling star in his hand, "is just the beginning. The first step is learning to see the light inside you."

He stood and slipped on his coat. "I have to go now, but I'll be back when you're ready for the next clue."

"Wait—where are you going?" Bexley asked, standing too. "And how will we know what to do?"

Grandpa pulled a small notebook from his satchel and handed it to his granddaughter. The cover was leather, and inside were pages of blank parchment. "Write down everything you feel when you think about Christmas: what makes it special, who you share it with, and how you can brighten someone else's day. Those thoughts will help you see the light inside yourself."

Thayer raised an eyebrow. "That's it? A journal?"

"Don't underestimate it," Grandpa said. "The answers will come when you start paying attention to the Christmas spirit already around you—and the spirit you create."

Before they could ask another question, he opened the door and disappeared into the snowstorm. The room felt strangely quiet without him.

Bexley and Thayer sat in silence for a moment, staring at the notebook and the glimmering star on the table.

"So," Thayer said finally, "what do we do now?"

Bexley picked up the notebook, a spark of determination in her eyes. "I guess we figure out what he meant. We follow the light."

Outside, the snow continued to fall, and far above the clouds, the North Star shone softly, as if guiding them toward a mystery far greater than they could imagine.

Chapter 2. The Journey Begins

Bexley woke up the next morning, the notebook Grandpa had left sitting on her nightstand. The events of the previous night felt like a dream— until she spotted the crystal star on her desk. Its light was dim in the morning sun, but the star was still twinkling faintly.

She picked up the notebook, running her fingers over the leather cover. Inside, the pages were smooth and blank except for the first one, where Grandpa had written a short message:

The magic of Christmas begins with your light. What does Christmas mean to you?

Bexley frowned, unsure where to start. "What does Christmas mean to me?" she muttered. Sure, it was fun—presents, decorations, big dinners with her family—but was that all? She flipped the notebook shut and stuffed it into her backpack, deciding she'd ask Thayer what he thought.

It was afternoon by the time Thayer arrived back home from the woods with their dad. By then, Bexley had reread Grandpa's note about ten times. Thayer came inside, his coat covered in snow. "Okay," he said, pulling off his gloves. "I've been thinking about last night all day. What was Grandpa talking about? And why is he telling us these things?"

Bexley shrugged. "He said it's because we're asking good questions."

"Yeah, but there's gotta be more to it," Thayer said, plopping onto the couch. He spotted the crystal star on the coffee table where Bexley had moved it and leaned forward. "That thing's still sparkling."

"Yeah," Bexley said. "It doesn't stop."

Thayer squinted at it. "Do you think it's a clue?"

"Maybe," Bexley said. She grabbed the notebook and opened it. "Grandpa left this, too. It says we need to figure out what Christmas means to us."

Thayer tilted his head. "That's a weird question. Everyone knows what Christmas is about. Presents. Cookies. Games. Family."

"Yeah, but what if it's more than that?" Bexley asked. She tapped the notebook. "Grandpa said Christmas is about following your light, or something like that. What does that even mean?"

Thayer thought for a moment, then snapped his fingers. "The library."

Bexley blinked. "What?"

"The library!" Thayer said, jumping up. "If Grandpa is for real, maybe we can figure out what he's talking about by looking up old Christmas stories. You know, the real ones."

Bexley hesitated. The library didn't seem like the most magical place to solve a mystery, but Thayer's excitement was contagious. "Okay," she said. "Let's do it."

The library was nearly empty when they arrived. A sleepy librarian sat behind the desk, flipping through a magazine. Thayer led the way to the children's section, where rows of holiday books lined the shelves. He pulled out a stack and plopped them onto a table.

"Let's start with these," he said, handing Bexley one with an old-timey illustration of Santa on the cover.

They flipped through books for over an hour, but nothing seemed to connect to what Grandpa had said. Most of the stories were about Santa delivering toys or magical reindeer flying through the sky. Thayer sighed, leaning back in his chair. "This isn't helping."

Bexley picked up one last book, smaller and older than the others. It was called *The Light of Christmas*. The cover had a simple drawing of a star shining over a snowy village. Curious, Bexley flipped it open.

The story was short and strange. It described a village where a bright star appeared every year on Christmas Eve, but only if the villagers had spent the season spreading kindness and joy. The star wasn't just a light—it was a reflection of their actions.

Bexley read aloud, "'The star does not shine on its own. It glows with the kindness of those who live beneath it, growing brighter with every act of giving and love.'" She looked up at Thayer. "Do you think this is what Grandpa was talking about? Like . . . the star is our light?"

Thayer leaned over to read the rest of the story. "Maybe. Grandpa did say the North Star is a symbol to follow."

Bexley set the book down, staring at the glowing crystal star in her pocket. "What if

Grandpa wants us to figure out how to make our own light shine?"

Thayer's eyes lit up. "Wait—what if that's the first clue? The crystal star is glowing but not very brightly. Maybe we're supposed to do something to make it shine brighter."

Bexley thought back to Grandpa's words in the notebook: *The magic of Christmas begins with your light.* "Maybe," she said slowly, "we have to do something kind. You know, like in this story."

On their way home, Bexley and Thayer passed their neighbor Mrs. Cynthia's house. She was out front shoveling snow off her walkway, her movements slow and stiff.

"She looks tired," Thayer said.

"Yeah," Bexley agreed. "Do you think we should help?"

Thayer grinned. "Let's try."

They grabbed two spare shovels from Mrs. Cynthia's porch and got to work. Mrs. Cynthia looked surprised at first, but then she smiled warmly. "Thank you, kids. My back's not what it used to be."

When they finished, Bexley felt a small spark of warmth—not from the cold but from knowing they'd made their neighbor's day a little easier. She slipped the crystal star from her pocket and gasped.

"Thayer, look!" she said, holding it up.

The star's light was brighter now, glowing steadily in the dim afternoon. Thayer's jaw dropped. "It worked!"

Bexley grinned. "It's like the story! It's brighter because we did something kind."

"Okay, that's officially amazing," Thayer said. "So, what's next?"

Bexley thought for a moment. "I guess we just keep figuring out ways to make it brighter. Grandpa said the magic of Christmas is about sharing your light. Maybe this is how we do it."

When they got home, they wrote in the notebook for the first time.

What does Christmas mean to me?
It's not just about decorations or presents. It's about sharing kindness and helping others.
That's how the light shines.

They closed the notebook, filled with a new determination. Whatever mystery Grandpa had set in motion, Bexley and Thayer were ready to solve it, one act of kindness at a time.

Chapter 3. The Hall of Mirrors

Bexley and Thayer were unstoppable over the next few days. They shoveled sidewalks, helped kids tie their skates at the park, and volunteered to sort donations at the community center. Each time they did something kind, the crystal star glowed brighter, its light warm and steady in Bexley's pocket.

But while they felt good about their efforts, they couldn't help but wonder what the bigger mystery behind all this was. And why had Grandpa not yet told them?

On the fifth night after Grandpa's visit, Bexley was sitting at her desk, scribbling in the notebook, when Grandpa called. He asked her to get Thayer and put him on the speaker. With both kids listening he said, "You've taken the first step. Now it's time to see the magic within. Meet me at the Hall of Mirrors tomorrow at noon. Follow your crystal star."

The next morning Bexley and Thayer, bundled against the cold, set out to meet Grandpa. They had never heard of the Hall of Mirrors and didn't know where it was, but the glowing star tugged gently in Bexley's pocket, guiding their way.

"I guess we follow it," Thayer said, his breath visible in the frosty air.

They walked for a long time, the star guiding them through snowy fields and quiet woods. Just when Bexley was about to suggest they turn back, they emerged into a clearing—and stopped in their tracks.

In the middle of the clearing stood a tall, circular building made entirely of glass. Sunlight reflected off its surface, creating a dazzling display of light. Above the entrance, carved into the frame, were the words:

✦

The Hall of Mirrors – See the Light Within

✦

"This has to be it," Thayer whispered.

Inside, the Hall of Mirrors was unlike anything they had ever seen. Dozens of mirrors lined the walls, but none of them reflected their surroundings in the normal way. Instead, each mirror glowed with a faint inner light, shimmering like sunlight on water.

Grandpa was waiting for them in the center of the room. "You've done well," he said, smiling warmly. "Your light is growing stronger."

Bexley held up the crystal star. "We've been doing kind things, like you said. But why does it matter? What's the point of all this?"

Grandpa gestured to the mirrors. "Let me show you. The Hall of Mirrors reveals the magic that lies within each of us. Step forward, and you'll see what makes your light unique."

Thayer went first, cautiously stepping in front of one of the glowing mirrors. The surface rippled, then transformed. Instead of showing

Thayer's reflection, it displayed scenes of his life: moments when he had helped others, laughed with friends, and stood up for what was right.

"This is . . . me?" Thayer asked, his voice soft.

"It's more than that," Grandpa said. "This is your light. Every kind act, every time you've shared joy or courage, adds to the spirit inside you. This is what makes your Santa Gene shine."

Thayer stared at the mirror, his cheeks turning pink. "I didn't think I was anything special."

Grandpa shook his head. "Every person's light is special. Yours shines through your sense of humor, creativity, curiosity, and your kindness."

It was Bexley's turn. She hesitated, then stepped in front of a mirror. The surface rippled and transformed, showing scenes from her life:

comforting a friend who was upset, helping her little brother with schoolwork, and laughing with him as they built a snowman last winter.

Grandpa placed a hand on Bexley's shoulder. "Your light is strong because you care deeply about others, and you're friendly and kind. That's why you were chosen. Your actions inspire those around you, even when you don't realize it."

Bexley stared at the mirror, feeling a mix of pride and wonder. "But what does this have to do with Santa?"

Grandpa turned to face them. "Santa Claus isn't just one person. He's the combined light of everyone who follows their North Star and listens to their True North—the part of them that chooses kindness, generosity, and love. This light is what we call the Santa Gene."

Bexley furrowed her brow. "So, the Santa Gene is what makes us do good things?"

"Not exactly," Grandpa said. "The Santa Gene is like a spark. It gives you the potential to shine, the choice to be warmhearted, but you choose whether to let it grow. Every time you do something kind, your light is strengthened. And when enough people share their light, the spirit of Santa becomes real."

Thayer's eyes lit up. "So, Santa isn't just a person. He's . . . all of us?"

"Exactly," Grandpa said. "Santa is a symbol of the Christmas spirit, an avatar for love in action, the best parts of humanity. And you two are learning how to keep that spirit alive."

Before they left the Hall of Mirrors, Grandpa gave them each a small pendant shaped like a star. "These will help you on the next part of your journey," he said. "The Hall of Mirrors showed you what your light looks like. Now, you must decide how to use it."

Thayer fastened the pendant around his neck. "What's next?"

Grandpa smiled mysteriously. "Your next clue will reveal itself when the time is right. Until then, keep listening to your True North. The light of the North Star will guide the way."

As Bexley and Thayer stepped back into the snowy clearing, the Hall of Mirrors shimmered and vanished, leaving nothing behind but the open sky.

That night, as Bexley wrote in the notebook, she couldn't stop thinking about what she had seen in the mirror. For the first time, both she and Thayer felt that the magic of Santa wasn't just a story; it was something real, something they could be part of. She wrote in the notebook.

What does Christmas mean to me?
It's about sharing my light, even when it's hard.
It's about choosing kindness not because I have

to but because it makes the world brighter. Being good for the sake of goodness—that's the real magic.

Chapter 4. The Reindeer Virtues

The days following Bexley and Thayer's visit to the Hall of Mirrors were filled with action. They continued finding ways to spread kindness, from shoveling driveways to visiting the local animal shelter. With every good deed, their star pendants glowed brighter. But Bexley couldn't shake the feeling that the deeper mystery of Santa's magic was still just out of reach.

As they walked through the park one frosty afternoon, Thayer asked his sister, "Do you think Grandpa will come back soon? I mean, we're doing everything he said, but there's still so much we don't know."

Bexley clutched the glowing pendant around her neck. "He'll come back. He said there were more clues, and I bet the next one will help us figure out why this is all happening."

Just as the words left her mouth, a soft jingle rang through the cold air. A gust of wind swirled snow around their feet, and when it cleared, Grandpa stood before them, his red coat gleaming.

"You've done well," Grandpa said warmly. "Your light is growing stronger. But to truly carry

Santa's magic, you must understand what drives it, the virtues that make it possible."

He led them deeper into the park, where the snow sparkled with an otherworldly glow. Before long, they reached a clearing. In the center stood a stable unlike any they'd ever seen, its wooden beams glowing faintly with golden light.

"This," Grandpa said, motioning to the stable, "is where Santa's reindeer live, not just as animals but as symbols. Each one represents a virtue that helps the magic of Christmas come alive."

Bexley and Thayer exchanged excited glances. "The reindeer are symbols?" Thayer asked.

"Yes," Grandpa said. "They represent the qualities that guide those who carry the Santa Gene. These virtues are what call us to action not just during the holiday season but whenever kindness and courage are needed."

Inside the stable, the air shimmered with a soft glow. Nine magnificent reindeer stood in a neat line, their eyes intelligent and kind. Grandpa walked up to the first one and smiled, gently patting its ruby nose.

"Rudolph represents courage, including the courage to shine. His glowing nose is a reminder that courage lights the way through darkness," Grandpa said. "Sometimes, being your true self is the most courageous thing you can do."

Bexley thought of the times she had stepped out of her comfort zone, even when she was scared. "Courage is harder than it sounds," she admitted.

"True courage often is," Grandpa replied. "But it's also what inspires others to find their own light." He moved on.

"Dasher represents the power of action. Wishing for something isn't enough. You have to take the first step, and then the next steps."

Thayer grinned. "That's like when we decided to help Mrs. Cynthia instead of waiting for someone else to do it."

"Exactly," Grandpa said. "Dasher reminds us that momentum begins with a single act."

The children enjoyed running their fingers through Dasher's thick fur before Grandpa called them to the next reindeer.

"Dancer represents joy and playfulness," Grandpa said, as the reindeer pawed at the ground. "Life isn't just about accomplishing things, it's about finding happiness in the journey."

Thayer beamed. "That's totally my favorite one."

Grandpa chuckled. "I thought it might be." He continued on down the line.

"Now, Prancer here represents the confidence to be yourself. I don't mean the kind of confidence that comes from being the best at something but the kind that comes from knowing and liking who you are."

Bexley thought back to the Hall of Mirrors, where she'd seen her own light reflected. "So, it's about belief in the good parts of ourselves?"

"Exactly," Grandpa said. "And confidence makes your light shine brighter."

He moved on to the next reindeer and gave it an affectionate pat. "Vixen represents the ability to adapt when things don't go as planned. One of the greatest gifts you can have is the ability to find magic in the unexpected."

Thayer laughed. "Like when we almost got lost on the way to the Hall of Mirrors?"

"Precisely," Grandpa said. "You adapted to the situation by trusting your crystal star to guide you, and it worked."

Vixen gave a short snort and leaned his great head down for Thayer to rub his huge antlers as Grandpa moved on to the next reindeer in the line.

"Comet represents positivity and hope," Grandpa said. "Even in tough times, a spark of optimism can light the way for others."

Bexley nodded and reached up to rub Comet's neck. "So when we do something kind we cause the star to glow brighter?" she asked.

"That's right. Positivity spreads, just like light." He smiled and moved on.

"Cupid represents love, the glue that holds everything together," he said. "Love connects us to one another and reminds us of what really matters."

Thayer touched his pendant. "That's what all our kindness has been about, hasn't it? Helping others feel loved?"

"Precisely," Grandpa said. "Love is at the heart of all the virtues."

He stopped in front of the last two reindeer. "Meet Donner and Blitzen," he said, holding out his palms for the two reindeer to nuzzle. "They represent strength and bravery when challenges arise. Sometimes you need thunder and lightning to push through a storm."

Bexley marveled at their enormous hooves and thought of the times she had stood up for others, even when it was hard. "It's not always easy, but it feels good when you do the right thing," she said.

Grandpa nodded. "And that's why these virtues matter; they are the foundation of our True North."

Bexley and Thayer turned around and walked back up the line, thinking about each reindeer's virtue as they ran their fingers through each one's thick, rough fur. When they got back to Rudolph, Grandpa turned to them with a knowing smile. "Now, you may wonder why the reindeer are said to deliver presents on Christmas Eve."

Thayer nodded. "Yes! Why is that?"

"It's because these virtues—courage, action, joy, confidence, adaptability, positivity, love, strength, and bravery—are what make the magic of Santa possible," Grandpa explained. "The reindeer represent the qualities inside people with the Santa Gene. These virtues call them to take action, to spread light and kindness, and to make sure that every gift—whether it's a toy, a smile, or an act of service—reaches those who need it most."

Bexley's eyes widened. "So, the reindeer don't actually fly through the air; they're symbols of the magic in us that delivers Christmas to the world?"

Grandpa nodded. "That's exactly it. When you live with these virtues, you become part of the team that keeps the Christmas spirit alive."

The children turned and looked at all of the reindeer once more, remembering the virtues that each one embodied. Before they left the stable, Grandpa handed them a small scroll. "This will lead you to your next clue. You've learned what the virtues mean. Now you must put them into practice in ways that truly challenge you."

As they walked home, the scroll tucked safely in Bexley's pocket, Thayer grinned and said, "I think we're finally getting it. The reindeer aren't just part of the story, they're part of us."

Bexley touched her pendant, feeling its glow against her chest. "And if we keep using those virtues, maybe we can help deliver the Christmas spirit, too."

Above the northern horizon, the North Star shone quietly, a reminder of the light they carried within.

Chapter 5. The Santa Gene

The next morning, Bexley woke with a sense of
excitement and curiosity. The scroll Grandpa had
given them lay on her desk, and the glowing star
pendant around her neck pulsed gently, as if

urging her forward. She didn't waste any time; after a quick breakfast, she called for Thayer.

"It's time to figure out what's next," she said, unfurling the scroll. The words shimmered on the parchment as Bexley read aloud:

The magic of Santa comes from within, but not everyone feels it. The Santa Gene is the spark that connects us to our True North. To understand its power, you must find those who carry it and uncover how it shines through them.

"What does that mean?" Thayer asked, frowning. "The 'Santa Gene'?"

Bexley stared at the words. "Grandpa mentioned it before. He said it's like a spark inside us that helps us follow our True North. But now we're supposed to find other people who have it?"

Thayer tilted his head. "Maybe we're supposed to look for people who are already spreading kindness and joy."

"That makes sense," Bexley agreed. "Let's start by looking around town."

The siblings spent the day walking around Central Point, observing the people they saw. Nothing seemed out of the ordinary at first: people were shopping, chatting, and hurrying through the snow. But then they began to notice small acts of kindness.

At the bakery, a man paid for an elderly woman's bread when she realized she'd forgotten her wallet. Outside the toy store, a girl helped a younger child up after he'd slipped on the icy sidewalk. And at the park, a group of kids built a snowman together, sharing laughter and teamwork.

"Do you think they all have the Santa Gene?" Thayer asked, watching the scene.

"Maybe," Bexley said thoughtfully. "Grandpa said the Santa Gene is like a spark. I think it's something everyone has, but some people let it shine brighter."

Thayer nodded. "So, how do we help people make it shine?"

As they walked home and pondered their next move, a familiar figure appeared on the snowy path ahead. Grandpa was waiting for them, his warm smile as bright as ever.

"You've done well," he said. "You're learning to see the spark in people. But the Santa Gene isn't just about seeing kindness in others— it's about helping it grow."

Bexley tilted her head. "How do we do that?"

"By sharing your own light," Grandpa answered. "When you act with courage, joy, and love, you inspire others to do the same. The Santa Gene is like a flame—it spreads when you share it."

Grandpa motioned for them to sit on a nearby bench. "Let me tell you a story," he said, his voice soft but full of energy. "Long ago, before Santa Claus was a person, he was an idea, a symbol of the best parts of humanity. Kindness, generosity, love—these qualities are in the Santa Gene. Everyone has the Santa Gene, but it doesn't always activate on its own. Sometimes it needs a little help.

"Over time, people who carried those qualities began to share them more intentionally. Their actions created small but powerful ripples of warmheartedness. That's how an activated Santa Gene works. It's the part of you that calls you to spread joy and give without expecting anything in return."

Thayer's eyes lit up. "So, Santa Claus is . . . *all of us*?"

Grandpa nodded. "Yes, that's exactly right. Every time someone with the Santa Gene acts from their True North, they add to the Christmas spirit. In that way, it's a part of Santa acting from the North Pole, directly below the North Star in the night sky. And that spirit is what makes the story of Santa Claus come alive."

Grandpa stood and brushed the snow off his coat. "Your next challenge is to activate the Santa Gene in others. Look for people who are ready to let their light shine but don't know how. Help them see what they're capable of."

Bexley frowned. "How will we know who's ready?"

Grandpa smiled. "Trust your instincts—and your light. The Santa Gene recognizes itself in others. You'll feel it."

He handed them each a small, glowing orb, like a Christmas ornament. "These will help. When someone with the Santa Gene acts from their True North near you, these orbs will glow brighter. Use them as a guide."

Bexley took her orb, feeling its warmth in her hand. "We'll do our best."

"I know you will," Grandpa said. "Remember, the magic of Christmas isn't just about giving—it's about inspiring others to give, too."

The next day, Bexley and Thayer decided to help sort the toys at the community center, where people were dropping off donations for the holiday toy drive. As they worked, they noticed a boy named Zak sitting alone by a window. He was one of the quieter kids at school, and he rarely joined in group activities.

"Let's talk to him," Thayer suggested.

Bexley was hesitant but nodded. They approached Zak and sat down. "Hey," Bexley said. "What are you doing here?"

"My mom's dropping off some clothes," Zak said, not looking up.

"That's cool," Thayer said. "We're helping with the toy drive. Want to join us?"

Zak shrugged. "I'm not really good at that kind of stuff."

Thayer smiled. "You don't have to be. Just come help us for a little while."

After a moment, Zak nodded and followed them to the sorting table. He worked quietly at first, but soon he began to smile as they joked about some of the sillier toys. When they finished,

Zak surprised them by saying, "That was fun. Do you think I could come back tomorrow?"

"Of course!" Thayer said, smiling.

Bexley felt a warmth in her pocket. She pulled out the glowing orb, which was now shining brightly. Thayer's orb was glowing, too.

"It worked," Thayer whispered. "Zak's Santa Gene is shining."

That evening, Bexley thought about Zak and the way his light had grown. She saw that the Santa Gene wasn't just about the big, magical moments—it was about the small connections that made people feel seen and inspired. She bent her head and wrote a reflection in her notebook.

What does Christmas mean to me?
It's about finding the light in others and helping it shine. The magic of Santa isn't just about what we do—it's about what we help others do, too.

Bexley looked up and saw the North Star twinkling through the window. She smiled. Their journey was far from over, but she knew she and Thayer were on the right path.

Chapter 6. The Secret of the North Star

The following days were a blur of activity as Bexley and Thayer worked to activate the Santa Gene in others. Whether it was encouraging shy classmates to participate in a school project or helping an elderly neighbor hang holiday decorations, their glowing orbs acted as a guide. Each time someone's light grew stronger, the orbs pulsed brighter and the star pendants around their necks shimmered in unison.

Something still felt unfinished, though. While they were helping others shine, Bexley couldn't shake the feeling that there was something bigger at play, something Grandpa hadn't yet explained.

That night, as the children wrote in the notebook, the phone rang. It was Grandpa.

"The time has come to unlock the North Star's secret. Meet me at the tallest hill in Central Point tomorrow at sunset," he said.

The next afternoon, Bexley and Thayer climbed the snowy hill overlooking their town. The sky was a swirl of orange and pink as the sun dipped low on the horizon. Grandpa was already there, waiting with his familiar smile and twinkling eyes.

"You've done well," he said as they approached. "The Santa Gene is shining brighter in Central Point now because of you. But to truly carry Santa's magic, you must understand one more thing about the North Star."

Bexley stared at the star pendant around her neck, then looked up questioningly into his kind face. "What is that, Grandpa?"

Grandpa smiled. "It's this: Santa's magic comes from the North Star. It's what gives him the ability to spread joy and kindness across the world. It shines through every act of kindness, every moment of courage, and every spark of joy. It's the light that connects us all, calling us to be our best selves. And it's what makes each of you part of that magic."

Grandpa pulled a small mirror from his coat pocket and handed it to Bexley. "Look closely," he said.

Bexley stared into the mirror. At first she saw only her reflection. But then the glass began to shimmer, and she saw the faces of everyone she and Thayer had helped: Mrs. Cynthia, Zak, the children at the toy drive, and countless others. Each face glowed with a faint light.

"These are the people whose Santa Gene you've helped activate," Grandpa said. "The North Star's light shines brighter because of them—and because of you."

Thayer leaned in to look. "So, every time someone chooses kindness, they're adding to the North Star's light?"

"Yes," Grandpa said. "And that light is what keeps the Christmas spirit and the avatar of Santa alive."

Grandpa turned to face them. "The North Star will always guide you, but following it isn't always easy. There will be times when the path feels unclear, or when fear and doubt cloud your inner True North. That's when you must remember the virtues that the reindeer represent."

He gestured above the northern horizon, where the first twinkle of stars were appearing. "The reindeer virtues—courage, action, joy, confidence, adaptability, positivity, love, strength, and bravery—are the foundation of your True North. When you have doubt or fear, or you're not sure what to do, look for your North Star. Your inner compass, your True North, will always find the way forward, the North Star will shine even brighter."

Bexley nodded, gripping her star pendant. "So, the reindeer aren't just symbols—they're the tools we need to keep the light alive."

"Yes, that's right," Grandpa said. "And now, you have one final challenge: to share what you've learned. The magic of the North Star grows strongest when it's passed on."

Grandpa reached into his coat and pulled out a small box, then handed it to Bexley and Thayer. Inside were two glowing crystals, similar to the one Grandpa had shown them when they first talked about the spirit of Christmas.

"These are seeds of the North Star," Grandpa explained. "Carry them with you and use them to inspire others. When someone is ready to find their inner True North and follow the North Star, the seed will take root, and their light will grow."

Thayer stared at the crystal in awe. "So, we're supposed to plant the light in others?"

"Yes," Grandpa said. "The Santa Gene is like a spark, but it needs encouragement to shine.

You've already begun that work; this is how you'll continue."

As the North Star became visible high above the horizon, Grandpa stepped back into the shadows and disappeared. Bexley and Thayer stood in silence, feeling the weight of the responsibility they now carried.

Thayer broke the silence. "So, what do we do now?"

Bexley looked at the glowing crystal in her hand. "We keep going. We help more people find their light."

"And maybe," Thayer added with a grin, "we'll make Central Point the brightest town on Earth."

The siblings laughed, their breath visible in the cold night air. Off in the distance, the North Star glimmered, its light a reminder of the magic they had discovered—and the journey still ahead.

That night, Bexley and Thayer wrote in their notebook, their thoughts clear and steady.

What does Christmas mean to me?
It's about following the light of the North Star and growing our True North, the part of us that knows what's right. It's about helping others find their own light and spreading the magic of kindness, courage, and joy. That's what Santa Claus is really about.

The stars were now gleaming through the window. Bexley and Thayer smiled and said good night to each other. The journey wasn't over, but they knew they were ready for whatever came next.

Chapter 7. Spreading the Light

The weeks leading up to Christmas flew by.
Armed with the glowing crystals Grandpa had
given them, Bexley and Thayer worked harder
than ever to share the light of the North Star. Each

act of kindness felt like planting seeds that waited to bloom into something magical.

As the holiday drew closer, so did the questions. Would their efforts be enough? Could two kids really make a difference in the world?

One frosty evening, Bexley and Thayer sat on the porch steps outside their house. The street was quiet, lined with houses glowing with Christmas lights.

Thayer sighed. "Do you think it's working? I mean, we've helped a lot of people, but the world's still, well, the world. There's so much we can't fix."

Bexley fiddled with the glowing crystal in her pocket. "I've been wondering the same thing. What if it's not enough?"

Before Thayer could respond, a warm light flickered between them. Bexley pulled out her crystal, and Thayer did the same. Both were glowing brighter than ever, pulsing gently.

"Maybe it's not about fixing everything," Thayer said, his voice soft. "Maybe it's about starting something."

Bexley looked at him, the light from their crystals reflecting in his eyes. "Grandpa did say the spirit spreads."

Thayer smiled. "Then let's keep going."

The next day was Christmas Eve, and Bexley and Thayer decided to do something big. They talked to all of the people they had helped over the past few weeks—Mrs. Cynthia, Zak, the kids from the toy drive, and others—and invited them to the community center for a special Christmas Eve event.

By early on Christmas Eve evening, the center was bustling with activity. Tables were filled with cookies, hot cocoa, and decorations. A small tree stood in the corner, its branches covered in paper ornaments the kids had made.

Thayer stood on a chair and clapped his hands for attention. "Thank you all for coming," he said, his voice bright and clear. "We wanted to bring everyone together to celebrate the spirit of Christmas—not just the presents and decorations, but the kindness and joy we've shared."

Bexley stepped forward, holding up her glowing crystal. "This light," she said, "isn't just a symbol. It's a reflection of what happens when we help each other. Every act of kindness adds to the Christmas spirit, and it's something we can all share."

The room fell silent as Bexley and Thayer handed out small paper stars to everyone. "Write down one kind thing you'll do this week," Thayer said. "It doesn't have to be big, just something that spreads the light."

Everyone wrote down the kindnesses they would do, then approached the tree one by one and hung their stars on its branches. As the tree filled, the room glowed with a warmth that had nothing to do with the lights.

Later that night, as the last guests trickled out of the community center, Bexley and Thayer stood by the tree, admiring the stars. Their crystals glowed softly in their hands.

"Do you think Grandpa knows what we've done?" Thayer asked.

"I hope so," Bexley said.

As if in answer, the room filled with a familiar warmth. They turned to see Grandpa standing by the doorway, his red coat dusted with snow.

"You've done something wonderful," he said, his voice filled with pride. "This is what the

Christmas spirit and Santa are all about—bringing people together to share their light."

Thayer beamed. "We couldn't have done it without you."

Grandpa shook his head. "You had the light inside you all along. I just helped you see it."

He stepped forward and held out his hands. In one was a scroll tied with a gold ribbon. In the other was a small, glowing object—a crystal shaped like the North Star.

"This," he said, handing the star to Bexley, "is for the people of Central Point. Place it at the top of your tree, and it will serve as a reminder of the light you've shared."

Bexley held the star carefully, feeling its warmth spread through her fingers. "Thank you."

Grandpa handed the scroll to Thayer. "This is for you both. It contains everything you've learned on your journey so you can share it with others. The spirit grows strongest when it's passed on."

Thayer took the scroll, his eyes shining. "We won't let you down."

"I know you won't," Grandpa said. "Your journey is just beginning."

That night, the glowing North Star crystal sat atop the tree in the community center, its light spreading through the room like a beacon. The paper stars on the branches shimmered, as if carrying the hopes and kindnesses of everyone who had hung them.

Bexley and Thayer stood outside, watching the light spill into the snowy streets. To the north, the real North Star glimmered dimly in the sky.

"We did it," Bexley said, her voice soft.

Thayer nodded. "Yeah. But it's not just us anymore. The whole town is part of it now."

Bexley grinned. "Merry Christmas, Thayer."

"Merry Christmas, Bexley," Thayer said. As the snow began to fall again, they knew that the spirit of Santa—the power of their True North—was alive and well.

The glow of the North Star lingered in the sky as they walked through the snowy streets toward home. The town felt quieter than usual, the kind of quiet that wraps around you like a warm blanket. It wasn't just the late hour or the snow muffling the sound; it was the magic of everything Bexley and Thayer had done.

As they approached their front porch, they paused to look back at the community center, now distant but still visible. The star atop the tree cast a faint glow into the night, a beacon of hope and kindness. They smiled. This Christmas had changed everything.

When they opened the front door, they were greeted by the cozy smell of pine and the faint sound of carols playing on the radio. Their family's Christmas tree sparkled in the corner, its ornaments reflecting the twinkling lights.

"Bexley, Thayer!" their mom called from the kitchen. "You're late! Come have some cocoa."

"Coming!" they shouted back, stomping the snow from their boots.

They hung up their coats and stepped into the warm glow of the living room. Their little cousins, Jaxon and Hayden, were sitting cross-legged by the tree, examining a brightly wrapped package.

"Finally," Jaxon said, looking up. "What took you so long?"

Bexley ruffled his hair. "We were just helping Santa."

Jaxon snorted. "Yeah, right. You're not Santa."

Bexley grinned. "Maybe not, but we're part of the team."

Later that night, as the house settled into its peaceful Christmas Eve rhythm, Bexley and Thayer sat with the crystal star, the one that started this journey, in their hands. The light pulsed softly, as if mirroring their heartbeats. They thought about Grandpa's words: *The magic of Christmas isn't just about giving—it's about inspiring others to give, too.*

The notebook lay open on the desk. Bexley picked up the pen, wrote two sentences, and then Thayer added two more.

What does Christmas mean to me?
It's about finding our light and helping others find theirs. It's about the reindeer virtues that make life truly magical: courage, action, joy, confidence, adaptability, positivity, love, strength, and bravery. Most of all, it's about

knowing we're all connected by something bigger than ourselves. That's what Christmas is, and that's what I'll carry with me all year long.

Thayer closed the notebook with a sense of peace, placing it next to the glowing crystal star. Tomorrow would bring more celebrations, more laughter, and more joy. But tonight, they rested in the quiet knowledge that the power of the North Star—that guided their True North compass and powered the magic of Santa Claus—was something they and millions of others carried in their hearts.

As the kids lay down to sleep, the North Star shone quietly outside their windows as if to say, *Well done.*

Chapter 8. The Bigger Reason for a Wish List

Bexley was sitting at the kitchen table nibbling on a Christmas cookie when Thayer burst through the door, clutching a piece of paper. His cheeks were flushed from the cold, and his eyes sparkled with excitement.

"You're not going to believe this," he said, dropping the paper in front of him. "It's from Grandpa."

Bexley picked up the note, its edges dusted with snow. The words shimmered faintly.

The next step is understanding Santa's Wish List. Meet me at the library.

When they arrived at the library, Grandpa was waiting for them in the quiet reading room, surrounded by shelves of dusty books. He smiled warmly as they approached.

"Ah, there you are," he said. He held up a blank sheet of parchment. "This is one of the most important tools in Santa's magic: a wish list."

Bexley frowned. "A wish list? Like what kids write to Santa?"

"Exactly," Grandpa said. "But it's not just for children. A wish list is more than a letter asking for toys. It's a tool for becoming crystal clear about what you truly want. Having that clarity is a skill that will serve you well your entire life."

Thayer tilted his head. "How does it work?"

Grandpa motioned for them to sit. "Let me show you."

He placed the parchment on the table and handed each of them a quill. "Start by thinking about something you want—not just something you wish would happen, but something meaningful, something that aligns with your True North."

Bexley hesitated, then wrote, *I want to help more people find their light.* Thayer followed, writing, *I want to bring more joy to the people around me.*

As soon as the words appeared on the parchment, they began to glow softly. Grandpa nodded in approval. "You see? When your wishes align with your True North, they become powerful. The magic isn't in the list itself, it's in the clarity it gives you."

Grandpa leaned back in his chair, his expression thoughtful. "When you're clear about what you want, you give yourself a direction. It's like a map for your journey. But the magic doesn't stop there."

He tapped the parchment. "A wish list also helps you focus on what truly matters. It cuts through distractions and reminds you of your purpose. When you act on those wishes—when you take steps to make them real—you create ripples of magic that can improve your life and the lives of those around you."

Thayer nodded slowly. "So, it's not just about writing down wishes, it's about following through."

"Precisely," Grandpa said. "The wish list is the first step. The next step is action—one of the reindeer virtues."

For the next hour, Grandpa guided them through the process of creating their own wish lists. He explained that each wish should be specific, meaningful, and aligned with their True North. He also encouraged them to include a mix of short-term and long-term goals.

"Remember," he said, "a good wish list isn't about asking for everything; it's about focusing on what truly matters. And it's not about perfection. Your list can grow and change as you do."

By the time they finished, Bexley had written down the goals of helping her cousins find their light and organizing another community event, which she really enjoyed. Thayer's list included learning to lead with joy and finding new ways to spread kindness at the activities he was a part of.

Grandpa smiled as he looked over their lists. "Well done. These wishes aren't just words on a page—they're the start of something truly special."

Before they left the library, Grandpa gave them one final piece of advice. "A wish list is only as powerful as the actions you take to make your wishes real. Each day, choose one small step you can take toward one of your wishes. Over time, those small steps will add up to something extraordinary."

Bexley tucked her wish list into her pocket, feeling a renewed sense of purpose. "Thanks, Grandpa. I think I understand now."

"I know you do," Grandpa said with a twinkle in his eye. "The magic of a wish list isn't just about what you receive, it's about what you create."

That evening, Bexley and Thayer sat by the window, wish lists in hand. They thought about how much their perspective had shifted over the past few weeks. The wish list wasn't just a tradition for kids; it was a powerful tool for anyone who wanted to live with intention and purpose.

Thayer picked up the notebook and wrote two sentences, then Bexley add a third.

What does Christmas mean to me?
It's about clarity, courage, and taking action.
The wish list isn't just a way to ask for things,
it's a way to focus on what truly matters. When
we're clear about what we want and take steps
toward it, we create magic—not just for
ourselves but for the world around us.

As the crystal star glowed brightly on the desk, Bexley and Thayer smiled. This Christmas, they weren't just going to make wishes—they were going to make them come true.

Chapter 9. The Mystery of the Coal

Thayer paced back and forth in the snowy clearing, his boots crunching in the frost. "I still don't get it," he said, glancing at Bexley. "Why would Santa give coal to anyone? Isn't that kind of . . . mean?"

Bexley shrugged, tightening her scarf against the chilly wind. "It's supposed to be for the kids who are naughty, right? Like, a warning or something?"

They were waiting for Grandpa, who had sent them a note saying he had something important to show them. He appeared as if on cue, his warm smile lighting up the winter morning.

"Ah, I thought you might be curious about the coal," Grandpa said, his deep voice full of humor. "It's one of the most misunderstood parts of Santa's magic."

Thayer crossed his arms. "So, isn't it just a punishment?"

Grandpa chuckled. "Not at all. Coal is a gift; a different kind of gift, but a gift nonetheless. Let me show you."

He reached into his pocket and pulled out a small black lump, smooth and glistening in the light. He held it up for them to see.

"Coal represents potential," he began. "It's a reminder that even when something seems ordinary or unremarkable, it holds incredible power within. Coal, you see, is waiting for a spark to transform it into fire—something warm, life-giving, and full of light."

Thayer tilted his head, studying the coal. "But why would Santa give this to someone? Wouldn't kids just think it's a punishment?"

"Perhaps at first," Grandpa admitted. "But coal is not about shame or blame. It's about opportunity. It's a way of saying that there is untapped magic within you, and when you ignite this magic and let it warm you, you become something extraordinary."

Grandpa placed a lump of coal in each child's hand. Thayer felt his piece. It was cool to the touch, but as he held it he felt a strange warmth, as though it carried something more than heat. Grandpa smiled knowingly.

"I am reminded of a boy named Jimmy Hyatt," Grandpa said, sitting down on a fallen log. "Jimmy lived long ago. He was known for making mischief in his village. He would play tricks on his neighbors, shirk his chores, and cause all sorts of trouble. One Christmas, Santa left a single lump of coal in Jimmy's stocking. Attached to it was a note that read, *This coal can either stay as it is or become something warm and bright. It can help you become warmhearted. It's your choice.*"

Bexley leaned forward. "What did Jimmy do?"

"At first, he was upset," Grandpa said. "But the note's message stuck with him. He kept that coal on his windowsill, and over time, it became a reminder to make better choices. The next year, Jimmy spent his days helping his neighbors— carrying wood for the elderly, sharing his toys with younger kids, and fixing fences. By the following Christmas, Santa returned not with coal but with gifts."

Grandpa took the coal from Thayer's palm and held it up. "Coal is not a mark of failure. It's a symbol of transformation. It says to the person receiving it that they have the power to spark change, to turn something cold into something full of life and warmth. Santa uses coal not to punish but to inspire."

He gave the coal back to Thayer, who looked at it carefully, his brow furrowed in thought. "So, it's like a message. A way to say, 'You can do better.'"

Grandpa nodded. "Exactly. Coal is a challenge *and* a gift. It's an invitation to see the potential in yourself and to choose a different path."

Bexley looked at her piece of coal and turned it over in her hands. "Does that mean we all have 'coal' inside us? Parts of us that need to change?"

"In a way, yes," Grandpa said. "We all have areas where we can grow, places where we feel stuck or not fully formed. But just like this coal, those parts of us hold incredible potential. With the right spark—courage, love, or determination—we can ignite something beautiful."

Thayer looked at his coal again, a small smile tugging at his lips. "So, it's not about being naughty or nice—it's about what you choose to do with what you're given."

"Precisely," Grandpa said, his eyes twinkling. "The power of coal is in its ability to transform. And that power is in you as well."

Bexley and Thayer walked home, each carrying the piece of coal Grandpa had given them. Thayer held his tightly, feeling its weight in his pocket. "You know," he said, "I always thought coal was just a bad thing. But now it feels different, like it's full of possibilities."

Bexley nodded, her pendant glowing faintly against her chest. "It's like Grandpa said. It's not about what it is, it's about what it can become."

"And what *we* can become," Thayer added, his voice thoughtful. He looked over at the North Star, shining faintly in the dusky sky. "I think I'm starting to understand. Even the simplest things can help us be better people, if we choose to let it."

Bexley smiled. "And if we choose to spark it."

That night, the kids placed their pieces of coal on the desk next to the crystal star and their glowing star pendants. They took turns writing in the notebook.

What does coal mean to me?
Coal is not about being good or bad, it's about potential. Coal reminds me that even the parts of myself I struggle with can become warm and bright. With the right choices, I can ignite a spark and create something extraordinary.

As the North Star twinkled in the distance, Thayer and Bexley felt a quiet sense of peace. This Christmas, they realized, wasn't just about the light, it was about learning how to create it. And with their coal in hand, they were ready to spark something new.

Chapter 10. He Sees You
When You're Sleeping

A few days later, Bexley and Thayer sat in the
library watching Grandpa turn the pages of a
thick, leather-bound book. The soft glow of the
North Star pendant on his chest illuminated his
kind face. "There's one line in Santa's story that

has puzzled people for a long time," he began. "*He sees you when you're sleeping, he knows when you're awake.* What do you think it means?"

Thayer frowned, thinking. "It sounds like Santa is spying on people."

Bexley nodded. "Yeah, like he's always watching. But that doesn't seem like Santa's style."

Grandpa smiled. "You're right, it's not. Santa doesn't watch over people the way you might imagine. The truth is far more fascinating. Santa knows whether someone has been naughty or nice because we *all* know, deep down, what's right and what's wrong. And we're all connected by something far greater than ourselves."

Grandpa leaned forward, his voice low and steady. "Every person has a conscience, a voice inside that helps them understand the difference between right and wrong. Some call it a moral compass, others call it intuition. We've been calling it our True North. It's that quiet feeling you get when you know you've done something kind or when you regret a choice that hurt someone."

Bexley's eyes widened. "So, when Santa 'knows,' it's because . . . *we* know?"

"Yes, that's it," Grandpa said. "Your conscience is like a mirror—it reflects your actions. And because we're all connected by the energy of the North Star—by something greater than ourselves—Santa can sense what's in our hearts."

Thayer tilted his head. "What do you mean by 'connected'?"

Grandpa opened the book in front of him, revealing an ancient illustration of people standing under a glowing star. "Throughout history, people have spoken of a universal connection that ties us all together. Some call it the Infinite Intelligence, others call it the Collective Unconscious, and still others simply call it love."

He pointed to the illustration. "This idea has been around for centuries. In ancient times, people believed that the stars themselves held the wisdom of the universe, guiding those who sought their light. Philosophers such as Plato wrote about an unseen force that connects all living things, and later thinkers such as Ralph Waldo Emerson spoke of an Over-Soul—a shared spirit that links us all."

Thayer's eyes lit up. "Like the North Star."

"Exactly," Grandpa said. "The North Star is a symbol of that connection. It reminds us that we're all part of something bigger, and through that connection, Santa can sense the choices we make. He doesn't need to spy; he simply feels the energy of our actions as they are reflected through our own conscience, our own True North."

Bexley leaned forward, intrigued. "So, the Naughty and Nice list—it's not about Santa judging us?"

Grandpa shook his head. "Not at all. The list is a reflection of what you already know about yourself. When you've been kind, generous, or brave, your conscience celebrates those choices and Santa feels that joy. When you've acted out of anger or selfishness, your conscience nudges you to do better. Santa doesn't need to decide; he simply connects to what's already there."

Thayer frowned. "But what about people who don't listen to their conscience? What happens then?"

Grandpa smiled gently. "Even when we ignore our conscience, it doesn't go away. It waits patiently, nudging us back to our True North.

That's the beauty of being aware of our True North—it's always there, ready to help us grow and become better."

Grandpa closed the book, his expression thoughtful. "When you understand this connection, it changes how you see yourself and others. You realize that the choices you make don't affect only you. They ripple out, touching everyone connected by the magic of the North Star."

He looked at Bexley and Thayer, his voice soft. "Every time you act with kindness, courage, or love, you strengthen that connection. You make the light of the North Star shine brighter. And every time you stray, your conscience is there to guide you back to your True North, helping you to realign with your best self."

Bexley nodded slowly, gripping her pendant. "So, when Santa 'sees' us, he's really just feeling what's already in our hearts."

"That's correct," Grandpa said. "And when you listen to your conscience, you don't just make Santa's job easier, you also make the world a little brighter."

That evening, Bexley and Thayer walked home and saw the steady North Star hung in its place in the sky. Bexley glanced at Thayer. "It's kind of amazing, isn't it? To think we're all connected like that."

Thayer smiled, his pendant glowing faintly. "Yeah. It makes you want to listen to that little voice inside, doesn't it?"

"Definitely," Bexley said, looking up at all the stars. "Because when we do, we're not just helping ourselves, we're also making the world a little better for everyone."

Back home, the kids sat by the window and took turns writing in the notebook.

What does it mean to be connected?

It means that every choice I make matters, not just for me but for the people around me. My conscience is my guide, helping me stay true to my best self, my True North. Through the magic of the North Star, I'm part of something bigger, something filled with light and love. That's how Santa knows, and that's how we all know.

As their crystals gently glowed, Bexley and Thayer felt a quiet peace. They realized that the magic of Santa wasn't about watching or judging; it was about connection, reflection, love, and the infinite intelligence that ties us all together.

Chapter 11. The True Santa Spirit Lives On

The morning after Christmas, Bexley and Thayer walked to their usual spot in the park as the snow glistened under a crisp blue sky. The town was quiet, the air filled with the peaceful stillness that follows a joyful celebration. They sat together on a bench, their pendants glowing faintly in the soft light.

"I can't believe how much has changed," Thayer said, looking at his star pendant. "It feels like just yesterday we were trying to figure out what all this meant."

"And now," Bexley said, holding her own pendant, "I think we've been part of something way bigger than ourselves."

Before Thayer could respond, the air around them shifted. A familiar warmth enveloped them, and when they looked up, Grandpa was standing before them, his red coat bright against the snow.

"This isn't the end of Santa," Grandpa said, his eyes twinkling. "It's just the beginning."

Grandpa sat down beside them, his voice calm and steady. "The magic you've discovered doesn't end with Christmas. The North Star's light shines year-round, guiding anyone who chooses to follow it. You've learned to see the light in yourselves and others. Now your task is to keep it alive."

"But how do we do that?" Bexley asked. "Christmas is over."

Grandpa smiled. "The spirit of Christmas isn't tied to one day or one season. It lives in every act of kindness, every moment of courage, and every spark of joy you share. Keep following your True North, and the magic of the North Star will follow."

Thayer frowned thoughtfully. "What if we make mistakes? Or forget to follow the light?"

"You will," Grandpa said gently. "We all do. But the North Star never stops shining, and neither does the light inside you. When you lose your way, simply pause, reflect, and trust the virtues you've learned. They'll guide you back."

Grandpa reached into his coat and pulled out a small leather-bound book. He handed it to Thayer, who opened it to find blank pages inside.

"This is yours now," Grandpa said. "Fill it with your own discoveries, your own reflections, and the stories of the people whose light you help bring to life. Someday, you'll pass it on to someone else who's ready to carry the torch."

Bexley took a deep breath. "Does this mean we're on our own now?"

Grandpa placed a hand on her shoulder. "You've never been alone. The North Star connects us all—those who came before you and those who will come after. Trust in the light, and trust in each other. And hey, remember that I'm your Grandpa!"

❄

Reflection Prompts

The magic of the North Star and the spirit of Santa Claus aren't just for stories; they're a part of you. The following prompts and activities are designed to help you to discover your own light, to follow your own True North—which is, in a way, living at your own North Pole—and to share kindness and joy with others. Use them to reflect on your thoughts and feelings, then take action and become part of the magic.

✦ Find Your True North

Think about a time when you felt truly happy and fulfilled.

* ❄ What were you doing?
* ❄ Who were you with?
* ❄ What values guided your decisions and actions?
* ❄ How did they align with your True North?

✦ Discover Your Santa Gene

Your Santa Gene grows brighter with every reindeer virtue you strengthen.

* ❄ What are some acts of kindness or generosity that you've done recently?
* ❄ How did you feel afterward?
* ❄ Who in your life inspires you to be kind and joyful?
* ❄ How can you pass that inspiration along?

✦ The Light in Others

When you see the light in those around you, the light in your own North Star grows brighter.

* ❄ Who in your life has shown you kindness or generosity?
* ❄ How did their actions impact you?
* ❄ Who in your life might need encouragement right now?

✴ How can you help them find their
light?

✦ The Virtues of the Reindeer

The reindeer virtues are courage, action, joy,
confidence, adaptability, positivity, love,
strength, and bravery. They represent the
foundational qualities of your True North
and help you be the best person you can be.

✴ Which reindeer virtues do you feel
strong in?

✴ Which ones do you want to develop
further?

✴ Think of a situation where you had to
rely on one of these virtues. How did it
help you navigate the challenge?

✦ Follow Your North Star

Your North Star is how your inner
compass—your True North—knows where

to go and what to do to be the best person you can be. Your True North holds all of your reindeer virtues, reminding you to take your best actions and make your best decisions.

❋ When you face a tough decision, what helps you stay true to yourself?

❋ How can you use your North Star to guide your reindeer virtues in the year ahead?

Activities

Doing activities to strengthen your reindeer virtues and your Santa Gene is fun and helps build your character as a good and kind person. Doing them together with friends and family will brighten your North Star and strengthen your True North compass.

✦ **Create Your Wish List of Kindness**

> Write down five small acts of kindness you can do for others this week. They could be as simple as smiling at someone or helping a friend with homework. Check them off as you go and then reflect on how each action made you feel.

✦ **Map Your True North**

> Draw a star map with your North Star at the center. Around it, write your True North values and strengths, and the names of people who inspire you. Use this map as a

reminder to stay aligned with your True North.

✦ Reindeer Virtues Challenge

The reindeer virtues are courage, action, joy, confidence, adaptability, positivity, love, strength, and bravery. Choose one of these virtues to focus on for a week. Each day, look for opportunities to practice that virtue. For example, if you choose courage, try something new or stand up for what you believe in.

✦ Star of Kindness Ornament

Make a paper star and write on it one kind thing you've done or plan to do. Hang it somewhere you'll see it every day as a reminder to keep spreading light.

✦ Write a North Star Letter

Write a letter to someone younger than you about how to follow their North Star. What advice would you give them? How would you explain the magic of kindness and courage?

✦ Family or Friend Reflection Circle

Gather your family or friends and share stories about moments of kindness or courage that made an impact on you. Reflect together on how you can keep those moments alive.

✦ Kindness Seed Journal

Start a journal to document acts of kindness you've witnessed or participated in. Reflect on how these moments contribute to the magic of the North Star.

✦ Find the Helpers

Look for people in your community who are spreading kindness—volunteers, teachers, and neighbors—and thank them for what they do. Write a note or give them a small token of appreciation.

✦ **Light-Sharing Celebration**

Organize a small event with friends or family, and have everyone share one thing they've done to spread kindness recently. End the event by turning on small lights to symbolize the North Star's magic.

✦ **Daily Reflection with Your True North**

At the end of each day, think of one moment when you felt connected to your True North. Write it down or share it with someone close to you. Over time, you'll create a collection of moments that remind you of your inner light.

✦ **Carrying the Spirit Forward**

The magic of the North Star and the Santa Gene doesn't end with the holiday season. By reflecting on your own light, embracing the reindeer virtues, and helping others shine, you'll keep the spirit of Santa alive all year long. Remember, even the smallest act of kindness can light up someone's world.

Now go forth and let your light shine. You are part of something bigger, and the world needs the spirit that only you can bring.

What is the Golden Christmas?

The **Golden Christmas** is a beautiful new tradition that honors the moment a child moves from a Believer in a solo Santa to someone who now part of Santa and carries the magic forward.

As you discovered in the book, it's not the end of believing—it's the beginning of being a part of something much bigger and deeper.

Now, instead of "breaking the news," families have a way to celebrate this important milestone with meaning, kindness, and joy.

Visit **BexleyAndThayer.com** to get **FREE resources**, including:
- A heartfelt **video message** for children experiencing their Golden Christmas
- A special **message for younger siblings** still in the believing stage
- Tips for parents and caregivers navigating this sacred tradition

Let's keep the spirit alive—together.

Acknowledgments

From the moment I first put on a Santa suit in 2003 the world has conspired to make me a better person. This journey has been filled with lessons, inspiration, and incredible support, and I am deeply grateful to all who have shared it with me.

To my wife, Lori, thank you for your unwavering wisdom and guidance from the very beginning. You've always been my compass, my True North, helping me stay aligned with what truly matters.

To my daughter, Danika, who appeared with me during my first seven years as Santa and continued to support me remotely while I was away from home. You've been working alongside me at the Worldwide Santa Claus Network since 2023, and I couldn't be prouder of the dedication and creativity you bring to this shared mission.

To my son, Zak, thank you for giving me opportunities to see and experience life in ways I never could have imagined. Walking alongside you as you've navigated the challenges of living with bipolar schizophrenia has profoundly broadened my perspective and deepened my understanding of resilience and compassion. Your journey has enriched my own in ways words cannot fully capture.

To my grandchildren, Bexley and Thayer, you are the light of my life. Your joy and curiosity inspire me daily, and working with you on videos has been one of the greatest blessings of my Santa career. Watching you two grow keeps me connected to the magic we all carry within us.

To the countless wonderful Santa and Mrs. Claus human helpers I've had the honor to connect with, mentor, and coach over the years, thank you for your dedication to spreading kindness, joy, and the Christmas spirit. Your passion and authenticity have enriched my life and continue to light the way for so many others.

To my longtime editor, Jessica Vineyard, who has steadied her inner compass to her own True North and follows her North Star all over the world, thank you for helping me spread happiness, joy, and love through your work on so many of my projects.

Finally, to the readers of this book, thank you for opening your hearts to this story and its message. My hope is that it inspires you to embrace your own light and share it with the world. Together we can keep the Christmas spirit—what I call love in action—alive.

With agape love and eternal gratitude,
"Santa" Ed Taylor

About the Author

Ed Taylor, affectionately known as "Santa Ed" and "That Santa Guy," began his journey as one of Santa Claus's helpers in 2003, when a friend became sick and asked him to fill in for a last-minute Santa appearance. What began as a single act of kindness quickly turned into a lifelong passion for embodying the magic and spirit of Christmas. Since that day, Santa Ed has made thousands of personal appearances as Santa Claus, spreading joy in homes, schools, hospitals, and events of all sizes.

Santa Ed has appeared in national and international commercials, TV shows, movies, and music videos, bringing the spirit of Santa to audiences around the globe. He has mentored countless Santa and Mrs. Claus human helpers, sharing his insights and experiences to help them bring the magic of Christmas to life. In 2015, he founded the Worldwide Santa Claus Network, LLC, an online hub for training, mentoring, and supporting Claus portrayal artists.

Beyond his work as Santa, Ed has spent decades as a professional speaker, marketing agency owner, and entrepreneur. He combines his expertise in storytelling and branding with his heartfelt commitment to spreading kindness and joy. Ed lives in Southern Oregon with his wife, Lori, and finds daily inspiration in his grandchildren, Bexley and Thayer, who often join him in sharing the spirit of Christmas.

Ed Taylor provided this book's vision, structure, and key ideas. Ed also had the creative assistance of ChatGPT, an AI language model.

The concepts, themes, and direction of the story were developed by Ed Taylor, who served as the prompt engineer, guiding the AI's responses to shape and refine the narrative. Through a collaborative process, Ed, ChatGPT, and the editing of Jessica Vineyard, the engaging storytelling, thoughtful metaphors, and structured content were brought to life in these pages.

This unique partnership allowed for the seamless blending of imagination, wisdom, and technology to create a fresh and inspiring take on the mystery of Santa Claus.

All images in this book were created using DALL·E, an AI-powered image generation tool. The visual concepts and prompts were developed by Ed Taylor, who served as the prompt engineer, carefully crafting the descriptions that guided the AI in bringing these illustrations to life.

Learn more about and stay up to date with Bexley, Thayer and their real-life grandpa, and author of this book, Ed Taylor at…

BexleyAndThayer.com

FREE RESOURCES

www.ingramcontent.com/pod-product-compliance
Lightning Source LLC
Chambersburg PA
CBHW031939090426
42811CB00002B/242